# Family Food
# For a Steal

## 50 simple, quick and delicious recipes

# Family Food
# For a Steal

50 simple, quick and delicious recipes

VINCENT SQUARE BOOKS

First published in Great Britain in 2011 by
Vincent Square Books
an imprint of Kyle Books
www.kylebooks.com

ISBN 978 0 85783 049 4

A Cataloguing in Publication record for this title
is available from the British Library.

10 9 8 7 6 5 4 3 2 1

Text copyright © various, see pages 124–5
Photography © various, see pages 126–7
Design © 2011 Kyle Books Limited

Design **Geoff Hayes**
Series Design **Nicky Collings**
Project Editors **Vicky Orchard and Estella Hung**
Production **Nic Jones and David Hearn**

Colour reproduction by Scanhouse in Malaysia
Printed and bound in China by C&C Offset
Printing Co., Ltd

# Contents

# Introduction

Cooking interesting and exciting food for a family of four or more can be a considerable challenge without even taking into consideration the obstacle of trying to do so on a budget. We all want to be able to cook delicious, thrifty food that satisfies the entire family, without spending hours slaving

away in the kitchen. This collection of recipes provides the answer – full of flavour these dishes make the most of ingredients that won't cost you the earth and show how cutting costs doesn't mean that you have to sacrifice on taste. These are simple and easy-to-prepare meals that the whole family can enjoy and what's more you can have them on the table quickly even after a hard day's work so everyone's hunger is speedily satisfied. Throughout the book there are suggestions for complementary mains and desserts, but rest assured that even these two courses will still add up to less than the cost of your average meal. There are also gluten-free and vegan dishes to cater for those with allergies or specific dietary requirements – throughout the book these are marked with a GF or V symbol to make them easy to identify.

Making soups is the perfect way of using up leftover or old vegetables and ensuring that you don't have to spend lots of money on expensive ingredients (Chapter 1). It also means

your meal will have the added bonus of being healthy for your waistline as well as your wallet – and a good step on the way to helping you reach your five-a-day quota. Soups are also proven to be one of the most filling dishes and beans are a great addition, bulking them out and providing a good source of protein at the same time – see Mexican Black Bean soup on page 22. Soups don't just have to be vegetarian to be economical – they are also a fantastic way of using smaller amounts of meat or fish, which tend to be the most expensive ingredients, and taking full advantage of the flavour only a little amount gives for a minimal cost. The Smoked Turkey & Lentil Soup (page 15) and Prawn & Pork Wonton Soup (page 19) are great examples of maximising the taste of meat or fish, while not breaking your budget by paying for a large quantity of these costlier ingredients.

Eggs are a storecupboard staple and provide a variety of options for meals throughout the day. A classic Eggs Benedict (pages 28–9) is traditionally served at breakfast or lunch, but is also a great option for a lighter supper. Omelettes and frittatas are a fantastic way of using up leftovers or whatever you find in the fridge – you needn't save the Full Breakfast Frittata (page 31) just for your first meal of the day and the Asparagus, Rocket & Wild Garlic Frittata (page 36) is delicious on its own or accompanied by a green salad for a more substantial dish. For something slightly different there's Tortilla with Chorizo (page 52) – a version of a Spanish omelette served in satisfying wedges. Eggs provide the base of sweet as well as savoury dishes and can be used to make pancakes for a quick and cheap dessert – see Blueberry & Banana Panckes (page 26) or for a change at breakfastime.

Pasta is an essential ingredient for creating tasty, filling and inexpensive family food. It's also the perfect option to feed a variety of ages as it's a dish that usually even the most fussy children will happily tuck into. You can use any type of pasta to provide the basis of the dish and add small amounts of other ingredients to provide the flavour, ensuring that costs are kept down. Spaghetti Puttanesca (page 64) is an Italian classic that can be assembled from mostly storecupboard ingredients, while Linguine alla Carbonara (page 67) is a creamily satisfying option for an evening meal. Pasta is also a brilliantly versatile ingredient as it can be cooked with a vast range of other foods and in different ways – baked pasta dishes provide a hearty alternative to a spaghetti or penne dish. Creamy Macaroni with Smoked Bacon (page 60) is a twist on the comfort food favourite macaroni cheese and you can use sausage or tuna instead of the bacon to make use of the contents of your cupboards, fridge or freezer without having to spend extra on any additional ingredients.

One of the simplest ways to make affordable food is to cut out the most expensive ingredients – often meat and fish, which can vastly increase the average cost of your meal. Vegetarian dishes can be just as filling and packed full of flavour, so you won't feel like you're missing out on meat. A Vegetable Curry (page 71) is a hearty and healthy option – helping to increase your family's intake of fruit and veg in one simple dish. Black-eyed Bean Casserole with Lime & Coriander (page 100) is a mouthwatering meal made from everyday veg like carrots and onions combined with tinned storecupboard standbys such as chopped tomatoes and sweetcorn. As well as curries and casseroles you can combine vegetables with pasta or with rice to make a tasty risotto like the brightly coloured Beetroot & Goat's Risotto (page 91) or a delicious stir-fry such as Stir-fried Rice with Avocado & Horseradish (page 88). Potatoes are another simple base for a vegetarian dish and much like a frittata a rösti is a good way of using up, and bulking out, leftover veg – see Potato Rösti with Mushrooms (page 84).

Cooking on a budget doesn't mean having to sacrifice dessert and there are lots of interesting choices for a sweet end to your meal (Chapter 5). As with vegetables, basing a dish around fruit can be an inexpensive and healthy way of feeding your family. Pineapple Kebabs with Vanilla & Maple Syrup (page 116) is a deliciously simple dessert and Blackberry & Apple Pears (page 119) is a perfect midweek sweet. Cakes aren't just for afternoon tea and a slice of Parkin (page 104) or Madeira Cake (page 107) will go down equally well after an evening meal. Combining bread and fruit like the Baked Apricot Brioche (page 115) or Strawberry Panettone with Fromage Frais & Honey (page 112) is another affordable way to make a tempting pudding.

# Soups

# Bubble & Squeak Soup

This soup is typically comprised of vegetable leftovers and is a great dish for a chilly winter's day.

Serves  4

400g potato, thinly sliced
1.2 litres chicken stock
150g thinly sliced streaky
   bacon
1 medium carrot, diced
½ leek, sliced
3 sticks of celery, sliced
1 medium onion, sliced
100g thinly sliced streaky
   bacon, cut into small
   squares
1 heaped tablespoon butter
½ small cabbage, shredded
100ml double cream
salt and freshly ground black
   pepper
sprigs of flatleaf parsley
   and sage

Simmer the potato slices in the chicken stock for 20 minutes or until soft. Meanwhile, preheat the grill to high and grill the bacon strips until crispy. Reserve.

Gently fry the carrot, leek, celery, onion and diced streaky bacon in the butter for about 15 minutes until soft. Blend the potatoes with the chicken stock until smooth, then pour in with the vegetables. Add the cabbage and simmer for 10 minutes.

Add the double cream then season with the salt and pepper. Garnish with parsley, sage and the crispy bacon.

# Smoked Turkey & Lentil Soup

The American love affair with the turkey goes back to the Pilgrim Fathers and long before. In this recipe, the smoked variety is combined with smoky chipotle chillies to produce a spicy and addictive soup which is, well, smoky.

Serves  4–6

8 tomatoes
3 tablespoons olive oil
250g smoked turkey fillet, cubed
¼ teaspoon mustard powder
1 teaspoon paprika
salt and freshly ground black pepper
1 teaspoon cumin seeds
125g celery, chopped
200g onion, chopped
1 red pepper, cored, deseeded and diced
1 yellow pepper, cored, deseeded and diced
4 chipotle chillies, soaked, deseeded and chopped
4 garlic cloves, chopped
½ teaspoon ground allspice
250g green lentils
2 bay leaves
1 glass red wine
1.25 litres chicken stock
1 tablespoon chopped fresh oregano
1 tablespoon chopped fresh parsley
1 sprig of thyme

Preheat the oven to 220°C/425°F/gas mark 7. Place the tomatoes in a roasting tin and sprinkle with a little olive oil. Roast them for 30 minutes, then blend in a food processor and reserve.

Heat half the remaining oil in a large, heavy pan. Coat the smoked turkey in the mustard powder, half the paprika and a little salt and black pepper and fry in the oil until brown. Remove with a slotted spoon and reserve.

Add the remaining olive oil and fry the cumin seeds for 2–3 minutes until they give off a nutty smell. Then add the celery, onion, peppers, chillies, garlic, allspice and the rest of the paprika and fry gently until the vegetables are soft.

Add the puréed tomatoes, the lentils, bay leaves, wine and stock and bring to the boil. Reduce the heat, cover and simmer until the lentils are soft, adding more stock or water if necessary. Finally, add the herbs and season to taste. Serve with the smoked turkey cubes sprinkled on top of the soup.

# Coconut & Chicken Soup

Chicken with coconut is always a winner, here backed up by that quintessential trio, chilli, garlic and ginger. You could pad it out with some cooked rice too.

Serves  4

2 garlic cloves, peeled
1 teaspoon chopped fresh
  medium-hot red chilli
2cm piece of fresh ginger,
  peeled and coarsely
  chopped
2 tablespoons groundnut oil
3 shallots, finely sliced
2 medium carrots, finely
  sliced
1 x 400ml can coconut
  milk
600ml chicken stock
2 chicken breasts, skinned
2 tablespoons fish sauce
a couple of squeezes of
  lemon or lime juice
½ teaspoon caster sugar
2 spring onions, finely sliced
fresh coriander leaves to
  serve

Place the garlic, chilli and ginger in a small blender such as a coffee grinder and reduce to a paste. Heat the oil in a medium-size saucepan over a medium heat, add the paste and fry it momentarily, then add the shallots and carrots and fry for a couple of minutes, stirring frequently, until nice and glossy. Pour in the coconut milk and the stock, bring to the boil and simmer over a low heat for 10 minutes.

Cut out and discard the white tendon on the underside of each chicken breast and thinly slice them across. Add the chicken to the soup and simmer for another 2 minutes. Stir in the fish sauce, the lemon or lime juice and the sugar. Ladle the soup into small deep bowls, with the chicken and vegetables in the centre, and scatter over some spring onion and coriander.

# Prawn & Pork Wonton Soup

This is extremely popular both in China and abroad, but often disappoints in Western restaurants, largely due to stingy stuffing of the wontons. No such problems with this version. Incidentally, wonton skins are a standard item in the fridges of Chinese supermarkets.

Serves  6

**For the soup:**
1.25 litres chicken stock
1 teaspoon fresh ginger, chopped
1 teaspoon chopped garlic
2 spring onions, chopped
soy sauce, to taste
fresh coriander leaves, to garnish

**For the wontons:**
300g minced pork
1 tablespoon soy sauce
2 spring onions, finely chopped
1 teaspoon sesame oil
1 egg white
pinch of salt
1 packet wonton skins (about 35–50)
250g prawns, small, peeled, raw (or cooked if unavailable)

Heat the stock in a large pan with the ginger and garlic and leave to simmer. Mix the first six ingredients for the wontons in a bowl. Place a teaspoon of the mixture on each wonton skin along with an individual prawn. Wet the edges with a little water, pull up the sides and pinch together, making a parcel resembling a miniature old-fashioned purse with the strings drawn tight. Bring a large pan of water to the boil and simmer the wontons in it until they float to the surface, the sign that they are done. Remove with a slotted spoon and drain.

Add the wontons to the simmering broth with the spring onions, and add soy sauce to taste. Simmer for a couple of minutes and serve garnished with coriander leaves.

# Miso Broth with Rice Noodles

Mix this recipe up with your favourite veggies; courgettes, sugar snaps, peas, all work; or try adding some tofu. You could even try a splash of Thai sweet chilli sauce.

Serves   Vegan

250g rice noodles
3cm piece of fresh ginger,
  peeled and finely sliced
4 tablespoons yellow, red or
  white miso paste
4 spears asparagus, sliced
  into 3cm pieces
4 baby corn, halved
1 carrot, thinly sliced
100g brown cap mushrooms,
  thinly sliced
150g broccoli florets
4 tablespoons chopped
  fresh coriander
50g beansprouts
2 spring onions, thinly sliced
1 tablespoon soy sauce

Cook the rice noodles according to the packet instructions.

Put 1 litre of water and the ginger in a large saucepan and bring to the boil. Reduce the heat and stir in the miso. Add the asparagus, baby corn, carrot, mushrooms and broccoli and simmer for 3 minutes. Add the coriander, beansprouts, spring onions and soy sauce. Cook for another minute.

Divide the noodles between 4 bowls and top with the vegetables and broth. Serve immediately.

# Mexican Black Bean Soup

The beans in question are sweet and wonderful in soups, and the sepia colour they give to this recipe is a reason for making it in itself.

Serves  4–6

2 tablespoons olive oil
200g shallots, finely chopped
4 garlic cloves, chopped
2 red or green chillies,
   deseeded and chopped
6 tomatoes, skinned and
   chopped
2 litres vegetable or chicken
   stock
250g black beans, soaked
   overnight and drained
salt and freshly ground
   black pepper
1 small bunch coriander,
   chopped
juice of 2 limes
200g grated cheese,
   to garnish
pinch each of ground
   cinnamon and nutmeg,
   to garnish

Heat the oil in a large, heavy pan. Add the shallots, garlic and chillies and fry until they have softened, then add the chopped tomatoes and fry for 2-3 minutes longer. Add the stock and beans and bring to the boil. Reduce to a slow simmer, cover and cook for about 2 hours, or until the beans are soft.

Blend the soup to a purée in a food processor, and season to taste. Stir in the coriander and lime juice and serve garnished with grated cheese and a pinch of cinnamon and nutmeg.

# Light Meals

# Blueberry & Banana Pancakes

A wonderfully naughty-but-nice snack for the morning. It's sweet but goes fantastically well with savoury breakfast fare, such as Eggs Benedict on page 28. And, in case you were wondering, these indulgent delights go equally well with lashings of maple syrup and a splodge of crème fraîche.

Serves  6–8

250g plain flour
2 teaspoons baking powder
pinch of salt
1 tablespoon caster sugar
2 eggs
drop of vanilla extract
1 ripe banana, mashed with
  a fork
about 300ml milk
a large handful of juicy
  blueberries
1 tablespoon vegetable oil
50g butter

Sift the flour, baking powder and the salt into a large mixing bowl and add the sugar. Make a well in the centre, crack in the eggs and start pulling in the flour from the sides. The slower you do this, the fewer lumps you'll have.

Add the mashed banana and start to add the milk a little at a time (you may need more or less, so keep whisking until you have the consistency you want). These are American-style pancakes and you want them to hold their shape in the pan so keep the batter on the thickish side. Lastly, throw in the whole blueberries.

Now heat together the oil and butter in a large non-stick frying pan over a medium heat. You should manage about three 10cm pancakes in each batch. Don't overcrowd your pan or you'll end up with one large, unattractive mess.

Take a large spoonful of the mixture and push it off the spoon into the pan. This is easily done with the aid of another spoon. Try to make them as round as possible. The blueberries will burst when they hit the hot pan so don't be surprised.

Cook for about 2 minutes or until bubbles start to appear on the surface of the pancakes. Flip over the pancakes and cook for a further minute. When they are ready, they should be golden brown and slightly puffed up.

Continue to cook in batches until all the batter is used. Your cooked pancakes will keep warm on a plate covered with foil.

# Eggs Benedict

Rich and gorgeous, this is often eaten for breakfast or brunch. The quality of the components can lift it from the mundane to the extraordinary. You can use smoked salmon, serrano or pata negra ham. This makes a great complement with Blueberry & Banana Pancakes on page 26.

Serves  4

**For the hollandaise sauce:**
1 organic egg yolk
½ teaspoon cold water
110g butter, diced
1 teaspoon lemon juice,
   to taste

**For the topping and base:**
a glug of sunflower oil
4–8 slices crispy bacon or 4
   slices cooked ham, slightly
   smoked, is good too
4 organic eggs
2 English muffins, toasted, or
4 rounds toast made from
   good-quality bread
a knob of butter

First make the hollandaise sauce. Put the egg yolks in a heavy-based stainless steel saucepan on a low heat, or in a bowl over hot water. Add the water and whisk thoroughly.

Add the butter bit by bit, whisking all the time. As soon as one piece melts, add the next. The mixture will gradually thicken but if it shows signs of becoming too thick or slightly scrambling, remove from the heat immediately and add a tablespoon or two of cold water. Do not leave the pan or stop whisking until the sauce is made.

Finally, add the lemon juice to taste. If the sauce is too slow to thicken it may be because you are excessively cautious and the heat is too low. Increase the heat slightly and continue to whisk until the sauce thickens to coating consistency.

If using bacon, heat a spot of sunflower oil in a hot frying pan. Cook the bacon until crisp. Drain on kitchen paper. Meanwhile poach the eggs (see below). Toast and butter the muffins or bread. Put 2 slices of bacon or 1 slice of ham on each piece. Top with the poached egg and coat with the sauce. Serve any extra sauce separately.

For perfect hollandaise you don't need a double boiler or any special equipment, just a good heavy-based saucepan and a little whisk. Once the sauce is made it must be kept warm. A Thermos flask can provide a simple solution on a small scale, otherwise put the sauce into a porcelain, Pyrex or plastic bowl in a saucepan over hot but not simmering water.

If you are making hollandaise sauce in a saucepan directly over the heat, it should be possible to put your hand on the side of the saucepan at any stage. If the saucepan feels too hot for your hand it is also too hot for the sauce. If you are making hollandaise for the first time keep a bowl of cold water close by you so you can plunge the bottom of the saucepan into it if it becomes too hot.

Hollandaise sauce cannot be reheated absolutely successfully so it's best to make just the quantity you need. If you do have a little left over, use it to enrich other sauces, enliven a fish pie, or beat it into mashed potato.

### How to poach an egg

No fancy egg poachers or moulds are required to produce a perfect result. All you need is a really fresh egg from a happy, lazy hen! Bring a small saucepan of water to the boil, add a little salt, reduce the heat, swirl the water, crack the egg and slip gently into the whirlpool in the centre. The water should not boil again but bubble very gently just below boiling point. Continue to cook for 3–4 minutes until the white is set and the yolk still soft and runny. Lift out gently on a slotted spoon, and drain thoroughly.

# Full Breakfast Frittata

This recipe is just superb for when you are cooking brunch for a large number. It will take you about 20 minutes to prepare, but once it is cooked, it can be left to sit in a preheated oven while you make the coffee. Pair this dish with a light, sweet offering, such as the Madeira Cake on page 107.

Serves  4

8 eggs
4 tablespoons olive oil
1 onion, sliced
150g potatoes, peeled
  and diced
4 sausages, cut into
  2cm pieces
100g smoked bacon
  lardons
8 cherry tomatoes, halved
sea salt and freshly ground
  black pepper

Crack the eggs into a large bowl, season with salt and pepper, and whisk lightly.

Place a 30cm frying pan over a medium heat and pour in 3 tablespoons of the olive oil. When the oil is hot, tip in the onion and potatoes, reduce the heat and leave to cook for 10 minutes, stirring every few minutes.

Once the potatoes and onion are cooked, add them to the bowl of whisked eggs, season with salt and pepper, and mix together.

Place the frying pan back on a low heat, add the remaining olive oil, tip in the sausages and bacon lardons, and cook for 5 minutes. Add to the egg mixture.

Put the frying pan back on the heat and, if necessary, pour in a small dollop of olive oil. Pour in the egg mixture. Leave to cook for about 10 minutes or until the egg mixture has set. Preheat the grill to high. Arrange the halved cherry tomatoes on top. Pop the frittata under the grill for 5 minutes or until it is golden in colour.

# Quiche Lorraine

Named after the Lorraine region of north-east France, this classic quiche is delicious served with a green salad and tangy relish. It tastes great cold, too. The sweetness of well-sweated onions is a fine addition. Serve warm with a green salad, followed by Blackberry & Apple Pears on page 119.

Serves  6

**For the shortcrust pastry:**
175g white flour, spelt or
  wholemeal flour, sieved
pinch of salt
75g butter
beaten egg or water, to bind

**For the filling:**
1 tablespoon extra virgin
  olive oil
175g streaky bacon, cut into
  1cm lardons
110g chopped onions
3 organic eggs
2 organic egg yolks
300ml double cream
1 scant tablespoon chopped
  fresh parsley
1 scant tablespoon chopped
  fresh chives
50g Cheddar cheese, grated
50g Gruyère cheese, grated
salt and freshly ground black
  pepper

First make the pastry. Sieve the flour and salt into a large bowl. Cut the butter into cubes, toss in the flour and then rub in with your fingertips. Keep everything as cool as possible; if the fat is allowed to melt, the finished pastry may be tough. When the mixture looks like coarse breadcrumbs, stop.

Using a fork to stir, add just enough beaten egg or water to bring the pastry together, then discard the fork and collect in into a ball with your hands, this way you can judge more accurately if you need a few drops of liquid. Although rather damp pastry is easier to handle and roll out, the resulting crust can be tough and may well shrink out of shape as the water evaporates in the oven. The drier and more difficult-to-handle pastry will give a crisper, shorter crust.

Flatten into a round, cover the pastry with clingfilm and leave to rest in the fridge for at least 15 minutes. This will make the pastry much less elastic and easier to roll.

Preheat the oven to 180°C/350°F/gas mark 4. Roll the pastry out on a lightly floured board until quite thin, then fit into a 23cm tart tin, bringing the pastry just a little above the rim. Line the tart shell with greaseproof paper and fill it to the top with dried beans to hold the paper in place. Bake for 20 minutes. Remove the paper and beans and save to use for another time.

Heat the olive oil in a frying pan and cook the bacon until crisp and golden. Remove and dry on kitchen paper. Then sweat the onions gently in the oil for 10 minutes. Meanwhile whisk the eggs and egg yolks in a medium-sized bowl. Add the cream, herbs, cheeses and bacon and onions. Mix and season.Pour the filling into the pastry case and return it to the oven. Cook for 30–40 minutes or until the centre has just set.

# Asparagus & Spinach Tart

A tasty take on a British favourite.

Serves  8–10

500g ready-rolled shortcrust
   pastry
2 large potatoes
125g fine asparagus spears
1 teaspoon ground smoked
   paprika
salt and freshly ground
   black pepper
50g Cheddar cheese, grated
250g spinach
3 eggs, lightly beaten
200ml double cream

Preheat the oven to 180°C/350°F/gas mark 4. Grease a 28cm fluted flan tin at least 4cm deep.

Roll out the pastry and use it to line the flan tin. Lightly prick the base all over and refrigerate for 30 minutes.

Place a piece of baking parchment over the pastry, cover it evenly with uncooked rice or baking beans and bake blind for 15 minutes. Remove the parchment and rice and continue baking for a further 5 minutes until golden.

Cook the potatoes whole in boiling water for 20 minutes or until they are tender, then refresh under cold water, peel and slice.

Meanwhile cook the asparagus stems in boiling water for 2 minutes. Remove and refresh under cold, running water.

Place a layer of potato, a pinch of paprika, seasoning and a sprinkling of Cheddar in the pastry case. Add a layer of spinach, a pinch of paprika, seasoning and a sprinkling of Cheddar. Repeat the layers.

Whisk the eggs and cream together, and pour over the filling, reserving a little. Arrange a line of cooked asparagus over the top and pour the rest of the egg mixture over the top. Bake for 20–25 minutes until golden.

**Tip:** Buy the best quality cheese that you can afford for this recipe – poor quality cheese has a tendency to turn oily and stringy when cooked.

# Asparagus, Rocket & Wild Garlic Frittata

Fritatta sounds much more exciting than a flat omelette although that's basically what it is. Unlike its soft and creamy French cousin, though, this type of omelette is cooked slowly over a very low heat during which time you can be whipping up a delicious salad to accompany it! This recipe is an example of how to incorporate seasonal ingredients into a frittata. Use a non-stick frying pan with an 18cm base, sloping sides and a 23cm rim.

Serves  6    Gluten-free

225g thin asparagus spears,
    tough ends trimmed
8 organic eggs
50g Parmesan cheese,
    freshly grated
2–3 tablespoons wild garlic
    and rocket leaves,
    roughly chopped
2 tablespoons olive oil
1 teaspoon salt
freshly ground black pepper
wild garlic and rocket leaves
    and flowers, to garnish

Bring 2.5cm salted water to the boil in an oven casserole. Blanch the asparagus for 3–4 minutes until just tender. Drain. Slice the end of the spears evenly at an angle, keeping 4cm of the tips intact. Reserve.

Whisk the eggs in a bowl, add the asparagus, most of the Parmesan and wild garlic and rocket leaves. Season with salt and pepper.

Preheat the grill. Heat the oil in the pan, add the egg mixture and reduce the heat to the bare minimum, using a heat diffuser mat if necessary. Continue to cook over a gentle heat until just set, about 15 minutes.

Arrange the asparagus tips on the top. Sprinkle with the remaining Parmesan. Pop under the grill for a few minutes, making sure the pan is at least 10cm from the element. The frittata should be set and lightly golden. Turn out onto a warm plate, cut into wedges and garnish with the wild garlic and rocket. Serve immediately with a good green salad.

# Cheese & Mushroom Soufflé

Originally a French dish, soufflé has become a firm British favourite. Here it's given extra bite with mature Cheddar cheese and English mustard. Pair this with another thoroughly British pudding, Parkin on page 104.

Serves  4

50g butter
40g plain flour
300ml milk
4 eggs, separated
75g mature Cheddar cheese, grated
50g button mushrooms, sliced
1 tablespoon chopped fresh chives
¼ teaspoon English mustard
salt and freshly ground black pepper

Preheat the oven to 180°C/350°F/gas mark 4. Lightly oil a 1.2 litre soufflé dish.

Melt the butter in a large saucepan, stir in the flour and cook for 1 minute. Remove from the heat and gradually whisk in the milk. Return to the heat and bring to the boil, stirring continuously until the sauce thickens. Beat in the egg yolks, cheese, mushrooms, chives, mustard and season to taste.

Whisk the egg whites until stiff, then fold a quarter into the cheese mixture, followed by the remainder. Spoon into the soufflé dish and bake in the preheated oven for 35–40 minutes until risen and golden brown. Serve immediately.

# Vegetable Puff Pie

Mushrooms, leek, broccoli and cheese make this hearty pie a meal in itself.

Serves  4

50g butter
40g plain flour
450ml milk
125g Cheddar cheese,
  grated
1 tablespoon chopped fresh
  parsley
pinch of English mustard
  powder
125g button mushrooms,
  halved and sautéed
1 carrot, sliced
1 leek, sliced and blanched
75g broccoli florets, blanched
250g ready-to-roll puff pastry
beaten egg or milk, to glaze
salt and freshly ground
  black pepper

Preheat the oven to 200°C/400°F/gas mark 6.

Melt the butter in a saucepan, add the flour and cook for 1 minute. Remove from the heat and gradually whisk in the milk. Return to the heat and bring to the boil, stirring continuously until the sauce thickens. Stir in the cheese, parsley and mustard.

Add the mushrooms, carrot, leek, broccoli, and seasoning to taste. Mix well and place in a lightly oiled pie dish.

Dampen the pie dish rim. Roll out the pastry on a lightly floured surface. Cut off a strip of pastry, and place on the rim of the dish and brush it with water.

Lay the pastry lid over the top and press the edges together to seal. Trim and flute the edges. Make a hole in the top of the pie to let out the air whilst cooking, and use the trimmings to decorate the pie. Glaze with egg or milk.

Place in the preheated oven for 30 minutes until golden brown.

# Crunchy Polenta Fishcakes

A real family favourite, these fishcakes make a great lunch or light supper.

Serves  4  GF  Gluten-free

125g brown rice
500g cod or other firm white fish
2 tablespoons crème fraîche
1 tablespoon finely chopped fresh coriander
1 tablespoon finely chopped fresh mint
juice of ½ lemon
salt and freshly ground black pepper
3 tablespoons polenta
30g gluten-free plain crisps, crunched up fairly small
1 tablespoon olive oil

Cook the rice in a pan of boiling water for 30–35 minutes or until very soft. Drain and set to one side.

Mash the fish, crème fraiche and rice together, or purée in a food processor, until roughly combined but not smooth.

Stir in the coriander, mint, lemon juice and seasoning. Cover and chill.

Mix the polenta and crisps. Divide the fish mixture into eight equal-sized portions. Shape each portion into a cake and roll in the polenta and crisp mixture.

Fry the fishcakes in the oil for 5 minutes on each side. Serve piping hot with a leafy green salad.

**Tip:** You can also replace the polenta and crisps with gluten-free breadcrumbs if you wish.

# Pissaladière

Serve this French pizza with Peperanata on page 47, if you like.

Serves  4–6

4 tablespoons olive oil
  (not extra virgin)
20 tree onions (or common
  onions, if unavailable),
  finely chopped
1 clove garlic, crushed
1 dessertspoon chopped
  fresh thyme
salt and freshly ground
  black pepper
360g once-risen
  bread dough
250g ripe tomatoes, peeled
  and sliced
60g canned anchovy fillets,
  drained and halved
  lengthways
16 large black olives, halved
  and pitted

Heat the olive oil in a heavy-based frying pan, add the onions, cover the pan tightly and fry, gently stirring occasionally for 15 minutes. Add the garlic and the thyme and cook uncovered for 15 minutes, or until the onions are reduced to a clear purée. Season to taste and leave to cool.

Preheat the oven to 200°C/400°F/gas mark 6.

Roll the bread dough directly onto a baking tray into a circle 25cm in diameter. Spread the puréed onions evenly over the dough, put the tomato slices on the onions and top with a decorative pattern of anchovy fillets and olives.

Bake for 5 minutes. Reduce the oven temperature to 190°C/375°F/gas mark 5 and continue to bake for 30 minutes or until the bread base is well risen and lightly browned underneath. Serve hot with a green herb salad.

# Peperonata

This is an indispensable stew. It can be used not only as a vegetable but also as a topping for pizzas, a sauce for pasta, grilled fish or meat, or as a filling for omelettes and pancakes. Serve it as a side with the Pissaladière on page 44.

Serves  8–10    GF Gluten-free    V Vegan

2 tablespoons olive oil
garlic clove, crushed
1 onion, sliced
2 red peppers
2 green peppers
6 large tomatoes, dark red
  and very ripe
salt, freshly ground pepper
  and sugar
a few fresh basil leaves

Heat the olive oil in a flameproof casserole. Add the garlic and cook for a few seconds, then add the onion, toss in the oil and allow to soften over a gentle heat, covered, while the peppers are being prepared.

Halve the peppers, remove seeds carefully, cut into quarters and then into strips across, rather than lengthways. Alternatively, cut the peppers flesh into 2.5cm squares. Add to the onion and toss in the oil. Then replace the lid and continue to cook.

Meanwhile, peel the tomatoes (scald in boiling water for 10 seconds, pour off the water and peel immediately). Slice the tomatoes and add to the casserole. Season with salt, freshly ground pepper, a sprinkling of sugar and a few fresh basil leaves. Cook uncovered until the vegetables are just soft, about 30 minutes.

# Quick Walnut & Mushroom Risotto

A great way of using up leftover rice, this is an easy variation on the classic risotto. Pair it with Strawberry Panettone with Fromage Frais & Honey on page 112.

Serves  4

2 tablespoons olive oil or
   25g butter
1 onion, finely chopped
250g large flat mushrooms,
   chopped
75g walnuts, roughly
   chopped
6 cloves
¼ teaspoon grated nutmeg
100ml white wine
salt and freshly ground black
   pepper
400g cooked long-grain rice
1 tablespoon double cream
 chopped fresh parsley, to
   garnish

Heat the olive oil or butter in a large saucepan, add the onion and fry gently for 5–10 minutes until it begins to brown.

Add the mushrooms, walnuts and spices and cook for 5 minutes, or until the mushrooms have begun to soften, adding a little more oil or butter, if necessary. Add the wine, season and simmer for a further 2 minutes until the mushrooms are tender.

Stir in the rice and cream and heat through gently, stirring constantly, until piping hot. Remove the cloves, if you can find them, and serve hot, garnished with chopped parsley.

**Variation:** The walnut and mushroom sauce is also delicious with freshly cooked pasta.

# Pasta with Ham & Vegetable Sauce

This quick and simple gluten-free pasta dish makes a great light lunch or supper.

Serves  4   GF Gluten-free

2 tablespoons olive oil
2 onions, finely chopped
4 celery sticks, finely
  chopped
125g mushrooms, thinly
  sliced
1 x 400g can chopped
  tomatoes
150ml vegetable stock
150ml dry white wine
1 tablespoon fresh marjoram,
  finely chopped
500g gluten-free pasta
50g cooked ham, chopped
salt and freshly ground black
  pepper
a few sprigs of marjoram,
  to garnish

Heat the oil in a heavy-based saucepan, and gently fry the onion and celery until soft. Add the mushrooms and cook for a further 2 minutes.

Add the tomatoes, stock, wine, marjoram and seasoning. Bring to the boil slowly and simmer gently for 20–30 minutes.

Meanwhile, cook the pasta until al dente according to the pack instructions, and drain.

Add the ham to the sauce, pour over the pasta, garnish with marjoram and serve immediately.

# Tortilla with Chorizo

This is take two on a Spanish omelette, that little bit more sophisticated than a frying pan affair and with it comes a little extra effort. It's one for serving at room temperature, so you can make it well in advance.

Serves   Gluten-free

4 tablespoons extra virgin olive oil
1kg medium waxy potatoes, peeled and thickly sliced
sea salt and freshly ground black pepper
5 onions, halved and sliced
a knob of unsalted butter
75g Parmesan, grated
9 medium eggs, whisked
100g thinly sliced chorizo

Heat 2 tablespoons of olive oil in a large frying pan over a medium heat. Add the potatoes and cook for about 5 minutes, turning them now and again to coat them in the oil. Season with salt, add 150ml of water to the pan, cover it with a large lid and cook over a low heat for 10–15 minutes, until the potatoes are just tender. Drain off any excess water and leave, covered, to cool.

Heat another couple of tablespoons of oil in a large saucepan over a medium heat, add the onions and cook them gently for about 20 minutes until they are nicely golden and silky, stirring them frequently. Season them, transfer them to a bowl and leave to cool.

Preheat the oven to 200°C/400°F/gas mark 6. Use the butter to grease a 20cm, 9cm deep cake tin with a removable base and dust it with a little grated Parmesan.

Season the eggs and coat the base of the tin with a few tablespoons of this, then use half of the remainder to coat the potato slices, and mix the rest with the onions. Lay half the potato slices over the base of the tin. Lay half the chorizo slices on top, then the onions, and then the rest of the potato slices. Lay the remaining chorizo on top, scatter over the remaining Parmesan and drizzle over a little oil.

Place the tin on a baking sheet and bake for 45–50 minutes, until golden on the surface and set – it should be no more than slightly wet in the centre when a knife is inserted. Run a knife around the collar of the tortilla and leave it to cool to room temperature. Serve it in wedges.

# Hearty Dishes

# Lemon Chicken with Lemon & Sage Risotto

A light and tangy main course that's quick and easy enough for a midweek treat.

Serves  4

4 chicken breasts, skin on
juice of 3 lemons and
  zest of 2
salt and freshly ground
  black pepper
1 tablespoon garlic olive oil
300g Arborio risotto rice
2 chicken stock cubes made
  up with 900ml boiling water
20g fresh sage, finely
  chopped
50g Parmesan, finely grated

Preheat the oven to 220°C/425°F/gas mark 7.

Place the chicken breasts on a baking tray, sprinkle over the juice of 1 lemon and season. Place in the oven and cook for 25 minutes.

Meanwhile, make the risotto. In a saucepan heat the garlic olive oil, then add the rice and stir to coat in the oil. Gradually add the stock a little at a time, adding more as necessary. Continue until all the stock has been used up. This will take approximately 20 minutes.

Finally stir in the sage, Parmesan, the lemon zest and remaining lemon juice, and stir to incorporate. Pile the risotto onto individual plates and top each with a chicken breast.

**Tip:** Replace the garlic olive oil with ordinary olive oil and gently fry 1 clove of garlic in it before adding the rice.

# Spaghetti with Chilli, Prawns & Parsley

For a really hearty meal, pair this with Baked Apricot Brioche on page 115.

Serves  4

3 tablespoons extra virgin
    olive oil
1 garlic clove
2 fleshy red peppers,
    deseeded and diced
salt and freshly ground
    black pepper
225–450g spaghetti
225g cooked, peeled
    prawns
red chilli flakes (optional)
175ml cream
2–4 tablespoons chopped
    fresh flatleaf parsley

Heat the olive oil in a sauté pan, add the garlic and peppers, season with salt and pepper and cover and sweat on a gentle heat until tender but not coloured.

Cook the pasta in plenty of boiling salted water. When it is almost al dente, add the prawns to the pepper, toss for a minute or two to heat through and add the cream and pepper flakes, if using. Bubble up and taste for seasoning. As soon as the pasta is al dente, drain well, add to the pan and toss in the sauce over the heat until well coated.

Turn into a hot pasta dish, sprinkle with chopped parsley and serve immediately.

**Variation:** Chunks of tuna or salmon may be substituted for prawns in this recipe, as can crispy bacon, kabanos or chorizo sausage.

# Creamy Macaroni with Smoked Bacon

This recipe is great for days when you want something that is comforting, tasty and quick to cook. Using spicy sausage or smoked tuna instead of the smoked bacon is also delicious!

Serves  6

500g macaroni
1 tablespoon olive oil
100g smoked bacon
   lardons
200g stale white bread
80g butter

**For the cheese sauce:**
70g butter
70g plain flour
650ml milk
200g Cheddar, grated
70g Parmesan, grated
sea salt and freshly ground
   black pepper
1 teaspoon Dijon mustard

Preheat the oven to 180°C/350°F/gas mark 4.

To make the cheese sauce, melt the butter in a heavy-based saucepan, stir in the flour and cook for 2 minutes until it resembles a small piece of dough. Slowly whisk in the milk, stirring all the time. Stir in the Cheddar and Parmesan. Season with salt and pepper, add the Dijon mustard and stir.

Turn down the heat and cook until the sauce starts to thicken (it should coat the back of a wooden spoon). The cheese sauce should be creamy in texture; if it becomes too thick, add more milk.

While the cheese sauce is simmering, tip the pasta into a large saucepan of salted boiling water and stir for about 30 seconds so that the pasta doesn't stick together. Cook for about 10 minutes, then drain.

Place a frying pan over a high heat and add the olive oil. Tip in the bacon lardons and cook for about 5 minutes until they are nice and crispy.

Pour the pasta into a 24cm baking dish, followed by the cooked bacon. Make sure that the bacon is evenly dispersed throughout the pasta. Pour the cheese sauce over the pasta.

Grate the bread (doing this rather than whizzing it in a food processor gives a better texture). Place the frying pan back over the heat and add the butter. Once the butter has melted, stir in the breadcrumbs and cook for 2-3 minutes.

Sprinkle the breadcrumbs over the cheesy macaroni and bake in the oven for 40 minutes or until the top is lovely and golden.

# Pasta with Sardines, Pine Nuts & Raisins

Purists would be very sniffy about the use of canned rather than fresh sardines in this classic Sicilian dish. But it tastes simply delicious. Incidentally, toasted breadcrumbs were once the poor man's Parmesan in Sicily.

Serves  6

350g spaghetti or tagliatelle
2 tablespoons olive oil
110g onion, chopped
50g pine nuts, lightly toasted
50g raisins, plumped in hot
  water
2–4 tablespoons chopped
  fennel leaves
2 cans best-quality sardines
  in olive oil
extra virgin olive oil, for
  drizzling
salt and freshly ground
  black pepper
6 tablespoons fine, dried
  breadcrumbs or 3
  tablespoons freshly grated
  Parmesan

Cook the pasta in plenty of boiling, salted water according to the packet instructions.

Heat the olive oil in a sauté pan, add the onion and cook on a gentle heat until soft and golden, add the toasted pine nuts, raisins and fennel and toss well. When the pasta is almost cooked, add the sardines to the sauce.

Drain the pasta, drizzle with a little extra virgin olive oil, add the sardine mixture and toss gently. Taste and correct the seasoning. Turn into a hot serving dish and serve immediately sprinkled with fine, dried breadcrumbs or grated Parmesan.

**Variation:** Substitute pan-grilled mackerel for the sardines.

# Spaghetti Puttanesca

This is one of the most delicious and convenient spaghetti dishes. And, should the occasion be a last-minute supper when a friend's dropped in, they are unlikely to feel hard done by.

Serves  4

400g spaghetti
3 tablespoons extra virgin
  olive oil
2 garlic cloves, peeled and
  finely chopped
6 salted anchovy fillets,
  sliced
1 × 400g can chopped
  tomatoes
1 small dried chilli, finely
  chopped
1 heaped tablespoon capers,
  rinsed
110g green and black olives,
  pitted and sliced
2 heaped tablespoons
  chopped fresh parsley
sea salt
freshly grated Parmesan to
  serve (optional)

Bring a large pan of salted water to the boil. Add the spaghetti to the pan, stir to separate it and cook until just tender.

Meanwhile, heat the olive oil in a frying pan over a medium heat, add the garlic and anchovies and cook for 1 minute, mashing the anchovies into a paste. Add the tomatoes and the chilli and simmer for about 7 minutes until the sauce is glossy and thickened, stirring occasionally. Stir in the capers, olives and parsley and cook for 1 minute longer.

Drain the pasta, but not too thoroughly, return it to the saucepan, add the sauce and toss. Taste for seasoning and add a little salt if necessary. Serve straight away. Add the tiniest sprinkling of Parmesan, but not too much.

# Linguine alla Carbonara

Bacon and eggs pasta – it's not difficult to fathom the appeal of this one, and equally not hard to imagine Anita Ekberg tucking into a plateful after dancing her way round Rome in *La Dolce Vita*.

Serves  4

1 tablespoon extra virgin
  olive oil
10g unsalted butter
225g unsmoked back bacon,
  rind and fat removed,
  sliced into thin 2–3cm
  strips
4 tablespoons white wine
450g linguine
3 large eggs
75g Parmesan, freshly
  grated, plus extra shavings
  to serve
3 tablespoons chopped fresh
  flatleaf parsley
sea salt and freshly ground
  black pepper

Place the oil and butter in a frying pan, add the bacon and fry until it turns crisp at the edges. Add the wine and cook for about 1 minute, then remove from the heat.

Bring a large pan of salted water to the boil. Add the linguine, stir to separate it and cook until just tender. Lightly beat the eggs in a large bowl, blend in the Parmesan and the parsley and season well. Drain the pasta, though not too thoroughly, and rapidly toss into the egg and cheese mixture. Quickly reheat the bacon, and toss the entire contents of the pan into the pasta. Taste for seasoning and serve straight away, with more Parmesan scattered on top.

# Chunky Ham, White Bean & Leek Casserole

Go to the deli counter at your supermarket and ask for ham ends. Sometimes they have them on display and sometimes not, but they are the odd nobbly bits that can't be used to make the perfect slice of ham when they carve the meat off the bone, so they never get used. They are brilliant and such a cheap way to bulk out an evening meal. Throw them into soups, pies or this casserole.

Serves  4

50g butter
3 whole leeks, trimmed and white parts cut into thin slices
2 x 400g cans cannellini beans (although any other white beans will do), drained
400g ham ends (or gammon steaks), cut into chunks
500ml vegetable stock
2 tablespoons cream cheese
2 tablespoons wholegrain mustard
salt and freshly ground black pepper
1 lemon
crusty bread, to serve (optional)

Put a flameproof casserole or saucepan onto the stove on a medium heat. Add the butter and then the leeks and cook them for about 10 minutes until they have wilted and softened. Keep stirring so they don't burn.

Add the beans and the ham ends (or gammon) along with the vegetable stock, cream cheese and the mustard. Season with lots of black pepper but take it easy on the salt as the ham will be quite salty; indeed, you might well find that you don't need any at all. Bring the sauce to the boil before adding a squeeze of lemon juice. (If you are using gammon steaks you will need to allow the stew to simmer for 30 minutes before adding the lemon juice to allow the meat to become tender.)

Serve in bowls alongside slices of crusty bread, if you wish.

**Tip:** This dish is just as good, if not better, the next day for a really warming lunch.

# Vegetable Curry

You can add chicken to this curry; if you do, just omit the aubergine. This dish always tastes better the day after it's made.

Serves  4  GF Gluten-free

500g potatoes, left whole if
   small and cut in half if big
50ml olive oil
2 onions, chopped
4 garlic cloves, crushed
5cm piece fresh root ginger,
   peeled and crushed
1 teaspoon turmeric powder
2 teaspoons cumin seeds,
   ground
1 aubergine, cut into wedges
18 French beans, cut into
   wedges
1 x 400g can chopped
   tomatoes
2 teaspoons ground
   coriander
3 tablespoons natural yogurt
sea salt and freshly ground
   black pepper

Half fill a saucepan with water, add the potatoes and place over a high heat. When the water starts to boil, reduce the heat, pour off half the liquid, and simmer until the potatoes are slightly tender. Drain the potatoes, leave to cool and cut into wedges.

Put a splash of the olive oil in a saucepan over a medium heat and add the potatoes, onions, garlic, ginger, turmeric powder and ground cumin seeds. Cook until the potatoes are golden, stirring all the time. Remove to a plate and keep warm.

Pour the remaining olive oil into the pan and leave to heat up before adding the aubergine and French beans. Cook for 5 minutes.

Return the spicy potato mixture to the pan and stir in the tomatoes, coriander and yogurt. Season with salt and pepper and leave to simmer over a low heat for about 10 minutes.

Serve with basmati rice.

**Tip:** If you can get your hands on fresh coriander seeds, then use these instead and stir them in just before serving.

# Naked Beef Burgers

Naked, purely because they have no salt and pepper. But you can add as much or as little as you want, if preferred. Try pairing this recipe with Pineapple Kebabs on page 116.

Serves  6  GF  Gluten-free

500g minced beef
  (15–20 per cent fat
  content)
3 tablespoons gluten-free
  breadcrumbs
salt and freshly ground black
  pepper (optional)
vegetable oil, for cooking
burger buns, to serve
  (optional)

The secrets of a good burger are to:

1: Use minced, or ground, chuck steak – 8mm mincing-plate size is perfect
2: Use meat that has between 15-20 per cent fat
3: And mince the meat twice, then mix together well, the meat will bind
    easier and the burger will hold its fat and moisture better.

Mix the beef and breadcrumbs well together, and add salt and pepper if you want to.

Roll into 6 equal-sized balls, and then flatten. Preheat the barbecue or grill to medium.

Very lightly oil the burgers on both sides; also lightly oil the barbecue rack using kitchen paper.

Cook the burgers for 2–3 minutes, then turn them through 90 degrees (this will give them an attractive criss-cross effect) and continue to cook for a further couple of minutes. Flip over and cook for the same amount of time on the second side.

Serve the burgers on their own for a gluten-free meal or in a bun for those who wish.

# Chicken Escalopes

A thin juicy escalope coated in crisp golden breadcrumbs with a squeeze of lemon and a smattering of parsley has to be one of the best ways of serving chicken breasts – strains of the Italian Riviera. Bettered only perhaps by a dollop of garlic butter melting over the top in reference to chicken Kiev. For family members who are still hungry, offer them the Banana Pizza on page 108.

Serves  4

2 skinless free-range chicken breasts
sea salt and freshly ground black pepper
100g fresh white breadcrumbs
extra virgin olive oil
lemon wedges and coarsely chopped fresh flatleaf parsley, to serve

Halve the chicken breasts into thin escalopes, cutting out the white membrane on the underside if it is evident. Season the breadcrumbs in a bowl, and dip the escalopes first in extra virgin olive oil, and then in the breadcrumbs, pressing them in. Set aside for 10 minutes.

Heat a couple of tablespoons of olive oil in a large frying pan over a medium heat and fry the escalopes in batches for a few minutes each side until golden. Serve hot or cold garnished with lemon wedges and chopped flatleaf parsley.

# Lincolnshire Sausages with Apples & Mushrooms

The great British banger served on a bed of fluffy mash. Perfect!

Serves  4

300ml dry white wine
450g Lincolnshire sausages
50g butter
1 onion, grated
2 crisp green apples, peeled,
  cored and sliced
150g button mushrooms,
  wiped and halved
200ml vegetable stock
2 tablespoons unrefined dark
  brown soft sugar
½ teaspoon ground
  cinnamon

Bring the wine to the boil in a large frying pan and cook the sausages for 10 minutes. Remove the sausages from the pan, discarding the skins and leaving the wine in the pan.

Heat half the butter in another frying pan and cook the sausages for 10 minutes, until golden brown. Add the onion to the white wine along with the apples, mushrooms, stock, sugar, cinnamon and remaining butter. Bring the mixture to the boil and cook until the apples are tender and the liquid is reduced to a thin syrup.

Serve the sausages with the apple sauce on a bed of mashed potato.

# Cottage Pie with Parsnip Mash Topping

A real family favourite topped with crunchy golden potato.

Serves  6

1 tablespoon oil
500g extra lean minced beef
1 onion, chopped
2 carrots, finely chopped
1 x 400g can chopped
    tomatoes
200ml beef stock
1 tablespoon tomato purée
salt and freshly ground black
    pepper
750g parsnips, peeled and
    quartered
4 tablespoons milk
25g butter or margarine
1 tablespoon chopped fresh
    flatleaf parsley (optional)

Preheat the oven to 200°C/400°F/gas mark 6. Heat the oil in a saucepan, add the beef, onion and carrot and cook for 6–8 minutes, stirring occasionally until evenly browned.

Stir in the tomatoes, stock and tomato purée and simmer for 20–25 minutes, stirring occasionally, until the meat is tender. Add seasoning to taste.

Meanwhile, cook the parsnips in lightly salted boiling water for 15 minutes or until tender. Drain and mash with the milk, butter or margarine and liberal quantities of seasoning.

Spoon the meat mixture into an ovenproof dish and top with the mashed parsnips. Place in the preheated oven for 20–25 minutes, until the topping is golden. Garnish with the parsley, if using, and serve with green vegetables.

# Beetroot & Horseradish Gratin

Rediscover the earthy, nutty taste of an old British favourite.

Serves  4–6

50g butter
50g plain flour
450ml milk
2 tablespoons crème fraîche
3 tablespoons horseradish
  sauce
300g cooked beetroot,
  chopped into large pieces
100g fresh white or brown
  breadcrumbs
2 tablespoons freshly grated
  Parmesan
salt and freshly ground black
  pepper

Preheat the oven to 200°C/400°F/gas mark 6.

To make the sauce, melt the butter in a saucepan, add the flour and mix to a smooth paste. Cook for 1–2 minutes, stirring continuously. Remove the saucepan from the heat and gradually blend in the milk. Return to the heat and bring gently to the boil, stirring continuously until the sauce thickens.

Stir in the crème fraiche, horseradish sauce and season with salt and pepper.

Place the beetroot chunks in an ovenproof dish, and pour over the sauce.

Sprinkle the breadcrumbs and Parmesan over the top and bake for 20–25 minutes or until the top is golden brown.

**Tip:** If you buy ready-cooked beetroot, make sure you buy the plainly cooked variety, rather than the sort that is packed in vinegar.

To cook your own beetroot, trim off the top leaves, leaving a small stump, and keep the root on. Wash the mud off, being careful not to break the skin, and boil whole in salted water for 30 minutes to 2 hours, depending on the size and age of the beets. The tops of young beetroots make an excellent addition to a green salad and have very pretty vein markings on the leaves.

# Vegetarian Delights

# Potato Rösti
# with Mushrooms

Rösti is a thick potato pancake of Swiss origin that comes in many shapes and sizes. It is served either with grated or melted cheese, soured cream, a savoury or sweet sauce, or on its own. Be sure to use a non-stick frying pan as potatoes are notorious for absorbing oil and sticking to the bottom of the pan. Pair it with The Dreaded Soufflé on page 111.

Serves  4

1kg potatoes, peeled and
   coarsely chopped
salt
50g butter or oil
2 eggs
225ml milk
pinch of freshly grated
   nutmeg

**For the mushroom topping:**
2 tablespoons butter or oil
1 large onion, finely chopped
400g mushrooms, sliced
2 tablespoons soy sauce
salt and freshly ground black
   pepper
3 tablespoons mascarpone
   cheese
juice of ½ lemon

Sprinkle the grated potatoes with salt and mix well. Heat the butter or oil in a non-stick frying pan and add the grated potato, spreading it out into an even layer. Fry over a high heat for about 5 minutes, cover, reduce the heat to a minimum and continue cooking for about 10 minutes until the potatoes are soft.

Beat the eggs together with the milk, sprinkle with nutmeg and pour over the potatoes in the pan. Cover and cook gently for about 10 minutes or until the egg is set. If the crust is ready and the top has not set, finish cooking under a hot grill.

Meanwhile, prepare the mushroom topping. Heat the butter or oil in a heavy-based frying pan, add the onion and fry over a high heat for 3–4 minutes until the onion is transparent. Add the mushrooms and soy sauce, and season with salt and pepper. Reduce the heat to medium and cook, uncovered, for about 6–8 minutes. Just before serving add the cheese and lemon juice and bring to the boil, mixing all the time. Switch off the heat.

To serve, turn the potato cake into a heated serving dish with the golden crust on top. Pour the mushrooms over and serve immediately.

# Leek Clafoutis

Clafoutis is the name of an ancient Gallic sweet, usually made with cherries, which is very similar to a fruit toad-in-the-hole. The fruit is added to a light batter flavoured with Armagnac and baked in the oven.

Serves     Gluten-free

750g slender young leeks, trimmed and washed
salt and freshly ground black pepper
350g fromage frais
2 eggs, beaten
75g Roquefort or Stilton cheese, grated or crumbled
1 tablespoon chopped fresh flatleaf parsley
butter for greasing
2 tablespoons hazelnut oil

Preheat the oven to 220°C/425°F/gas mark 7.

Cook the leeks in plenty of boiling salted water for 10–12 minutes, then drain well. Alternatively steam the leeks for 10 minutes. Meanwhile, mix the fromage frais with the eggs, half the cheese, salt, pepper and parsley.

Butter an ovenproof dish and pour in with half the egg and cheese mixture. Lay the well-drained leeks on top and cover with the remaining sauce. Dot with the remaining cheese and sprinkle with the oil.

Bake in the pre-heated oven for 15 minutes. Serve either hot or at room temperature, accompanied by a green salad and a glass of chilled dry white wine such as Muscadet.

# Stir-fried Rice with Avocado & Horseradish

Fried rice with a difference – quick, easy and filling.

Serves  4 GF Gluten-free

2 x 115g packs
  microwaveable basmati
  rice
2 large tomatoes, chopped
1 ripe avocado, cubed
4 tablespoons chopped fresh
  coriander
2 spring onions, sliced
  diagonally
1–2 tablespoons vegetable
  oil
salt and freshly ground black
  pepper
2 large eggs, beaten
1 tablespoon creamed
  horseradish

Cook the rice in the microwave according to the packet instructions.

Place the tomatoes, avocado, coriander and spring onions in a serving dish and mix well.

Heat the oil in a wok, add the cooked rice and stir well.

Add the beaten eggs and mix well until the eggs are cooked. Season well with salt and pepper.

Tip the rice onto the tomato mixture, season well and stir in the creamed horseradish. Serve straight away, whilst hot.

# Beetroot & Goat's Cheese Risotto

This is probably the most outrageously coloured plate of food you will ever cook!

Serves  4

2 large beetroot
50g butter
2 shallots, finely chopped
1 leek, white part only,
   finely chopped
1 garlic clove, chopped
sprig of thyme, leaves only
350g Arborio rice
150ml white wine
1 litre hot vegetable stock
150g goat's cheese,
   crumbled
75g Parmesan, finely grated

Peel and dice the beetroot as small as you can.

Melt the butter in a shallow-sided pan and add the shallot, leek, garlic and diced beetroot. Cook them slowly and allow the shallots and leeks to go translucent. Once this has happened, add the thyme and rice. Turn the rice over in the now purple ingredients and ensure that every grain is coated in the butter.

Turn up the heat slightly and add the white wine. Keep the rice moving at all times. When the liquid has all been absorbed, add a ladleful of hot stock. Continue to add a ladleful at a time, stirring to keep the rice constantly on the move. This takes about 15 minutes.

When the rice is just under done, add the goat's cheese and the Parmesan. Correct the seasoning with salt, if necessary, remove the thyme stalk and serve.

# Butternut Squash &
# Barley Risotto

One of the best things about this dish is the stock; there is so much flavour in the squash skins. Whenever you use a squash, make a stock and freeze it.

Serves  4

**For the butternut squash stock:**
2 tablespoons olive oil
1 Spanish onion
1 large butternut squash
1 bay leaf
1 cinnamon stick
1 carrot
3 garlic cloves

**For the risotto:**
1 peeled butternut squash,
   from above
50ml olive oil
salt and freshly ground
   black pepper
pinch of nutmeg
2 shallots, diced
1 teaspoon ground cumin
400g pearl barley
100ml dry white wine
1 litre hot squash stock
juice and finely grated zest
   of 1 lemon
60g fresh Parmesan, grated
2 tablespoons chopped fresh
   mint leaves
40ml pumpkin seed oil
rocket salad, to serve

To make the stock: in a large pan, heat the olive oil. Halve and slice the onion, leaving the skin on and cook over a high heat for 2 minutes. Peel the squash and add the peelings to the pan, along with the bay leaf, cinnamon, carrot and garlic. Continue to cook over a high heat for a further 2 minutes. Cut the top half from the squash and cut the bulbous part in half lengthways. Scoop out the seeds and add these to the stock. Add 2.5 litres of water, bring to the boil, then reduce to a simmer and cook for 30 minutes. Strain and return to the pan, if using for risotto straight away. Otherwise leave to cool, then refrigerate or freeze.

Preheat the oven 180°C/350°F/gas mark 4. Cut the top half of the squash into 1cm dice and set aside; cut the bulbous half into rough 2cm chunks. Place the chunks of squash on a roasting tray, drizzle with olive oil, season with salt, pepper and a little grated nutmeg and roast until softened, about 20 minutes. Remove from the oven and purée until smooth.

Meanwhile, heat the remaining olive oil in a large pan and, once hot, add the shallots, cumin and diced squash. Cook over a medium heat until golden. Add the barley and cook for 1 minute, stirring constantly. Add the wine and allow the barley to absorb all the liquid. Repeat with a large ladleful of hot squash stock, making sure it is absorbed before adding the next. Cook until the barley is tender and most of the stock has been absorbed, about 30 minutes.

Stir in the squash purée and warm through, then remove from the heat and add the lemon zest and juice to taste, Parmesan and mint. Check the seasoning and drizzle with pumpkin seed oil. Serve with a rocket salad.

# Fettucine with Spinach, Mushroom & Goat's Cheese

Fresh goat's cheese (British or French) melted with crème fraîche makes a delicious creamy sauce for pasta, much tastier than double cream alone.

Serves  4

100g unsalted butter
2 shallots, finely chopped
1 clove of garlic, finely
   chopped
275g chestnut button
mushrooms, washed
   and sliced
juice of ½ lemon
salt and freshly ground
   black pepper
2 tablespoons crème fraîche
100g goat's cheese, cut
   into small chunks
170g baby spinach, washed,
   drained and roughly
   chopped
400g fettucine (ribbon
   noodles)

Bring a large saucepan of salted water to the boil and cook the fettucine according to the packet instructions.

Meanwhile, melt the butter in a frying pan. When it begins to sizzle, add the shallots and garlic and leave to colour for a couple minutes, then add the mushrooms and lemon juice. Season and cook until most of the juice has evaporated.

Spoon the crème fraîche and goat's cheese into the pan. Leave to simmer over a low heat, stirring occasionally, until the cheese has melted, then add the spinach and leave to wilt in the sauce.

When the fettucine is ready, drain well, then toss in the sauce and serve with a final sprinkling of freshly ground black pepper.

# Courgette, Basil & Chilli Linguine with Crème Fraîche

A healthy and tasty meal that can be prepared in minutes. You don't need to resort to takeaway or pre-made dinners – this dish can be on the table within 20 minutes of walking through the door. Try adding cooked ham and a few fresh peas when in season.

Serves  4

salt and freshly ground
  black pepper
500g dried linguine
2 tablespoons olive oil, plus
  extra to drizzle
½ teaspoon chilli flakes
2 garlic cloves, chopped
4 large courgettes, roughly
  grated
juice of 1 lemon
15 basil leaves
4–5 tablespoons crème
  fraîche
100g Parmesan, grated

Put a big pan of water on the stove to boil and add a pinch of salt. When the water starts to boil, add the pasta and cook according to the packet instructions until al dente.

Meanwhile, heat the olive oil in a small pan on a very low heat with the chilli flakes and garlic. Turn off the heat once they start to cook and bubble.

Drain the pasta and add back into the pan it was cooked in. Stir in the chilli, garlic and warmed olive oil. Then add the courgettes, lemon juice and basil and stir through the crème fraîche. Season well with salt and pepper.

Serve with a drizzle of olive oil and the grated Parmesan cheese.

# Conchiglie with Butternut Squash & Sage Butter

A butternut squash in the vegetable basket is a great standby. They last almost indefinitely, which makes this pasta dish a regular meal. And as ever, the pasta shape should be governed by what's in the cupboard.

Serves  4

2 butternut squash (about 800g each)
3 tablespoons extra virgin olive oil
sea salt and freshly ground black pepper
4 garlic cloves, sliced
300g conchiglie
100g unsalted butter
10g fresh sage leaves
freshly grated Parmesan to serve

Preheat the oven to 200°C/400°F/gas mark 6. Cut the skin off the squash, quarter the bulbous part to remove the seeds and slice these sections into wedges. Halve the remaining cylindrical trunks lengthwise and slice 1cm thick. Arrange the squash in a crowded single layer in a baking tray (38 × 25cm). Drizzle over the olive oil, season and roast for 50–55 minutes, turning the squash after 25 minutes. Scatter the garlic over the squash and give everything another stir 15 minutes before the end.

Halfway through cooking the squash, bring a large pan of salted water to the boil. Add the conchiglie, stir and cook until just tender – most dried varieties take about 10 minutes.

Five minutes before the pasta is due to be ready, melt the butter in a medium-size frying pan over a medium heat. Skim off the surface foam, decant the clarified butter into a bowl and discard the milky residue in the base. Return the clarified butter to the pan and heat, scattering the sage leaves over the surface. Cook until they darken in colour and crisp, then remove from the heat.

Drain the pasta, add it to the roasting pan and gently turn, using a spatula, to coat with the oil and sticky roasting juices. Spoon the butter and sage leaves on top, scatter over some more seasoning and gently toss again. Serve accompanied by the Parmesan.

# Black-eyed Bean Casserole with Lime & Coriander

A healthy vegetarian style dish with a delicious mix of herbs and spices.

Serves  4  GF Gluten-free

**For the casserole:**
250g black-eyed beans
2 tablespoons sunflower oil
1 onion, finely chopped
2 garlic cloves, finely
  chopped
1 tablespoon paprika
1 bird's eye chilli, deseeded
  and finely chopped
125g carrots, peeled and cut
  into 1cm dice
1 x 400g can chopped
  tomatoes
1 x 325g can sweetcorn
dash of Tabasco
a handful of fresh coriander,
  finely chopped
salt and freshly ground
  black pepper

**For the lime and coriander
cream (optional):**
125ml soured cream
a handful of fresh coriander,
  roughly chopped
1 tablespoon lime juice

To make the casserole, soak the black-eyed beans in water overnight, drain and boil in plenty of water until tender, approximately 45 minutes.

Heat the oil in a pan and cook the onion until golden brown. Add the garlic just as the onions are browning.

Add the paprika, chilli and carrots and cook slowly until the carrots are 'al dente'. The mixture in the pan will resemble a thick paste.

Pour in the can of tomatoes and drained black-eyed beans and simmer gently for 5 minutes.

Add the sweetcorn, a dash of Tabasco and seasoning, continue to simmer for 6-7 minutes, making sure that it does not dry out. Remove from the heat and sprinkle over the coriander.

For the lime and coriander cream, mix together the soured cream, coriander and lime juice. Season to taste before serving with the casserole.

# Sweet Endings

# Parkin

This sticky cake is now as much a part of Bonfire Night as Guy Fawkes himself. Pair this with the Cheese and Mushroom Soufflé on page 39.

Serves  12

175g golden syrup
100g black treacle
75g light muscovado sugar
175g unsalted butter
200g oatmeal
250g plain flour
1 teaspoon ground ginger
2 teaspoons bicarbonate
  of soda
1 egg, beaten with 3
  tablespoons milk

Preheat the oven to 160°C/325°F/gas mark 3. Line a 23cm square tin with baking parchment, including the sides.

Put the syrup, treacle, sugar and butter in a saucepan and dissolve together. Put to one side when well mixed.

Mix together the oatmeal, flour, ginger and bicarbonate of soda and stir into the syrup, followed by the egg and milk.

Pour into the prepared tin and bake for 1 hour, or until an inserted skewer comes out clean. Transfer to a wire rack, remove the paper and allow to cool. Cut into 12 pieces.

# Madeira Cake

This traditional light and buttery English cake makes a delicious brunch companion with the Full Breakfast Frittata on page 31.

Serves  6–8

115g unsalted butter, softened
115g caster sugar
zest of 1 lemon
200g self-raising flour, sifted
2 eggs, beaten
thinly sliced candied lemon peel

Preheat the oven to 160°C/325°F/gas mark 3. Grease and line a 454g loaf tin.

Cream the butter and sugar together until light and fluffy, then beat in the lemon zest.

Stir in the flour and eggs, alternately, a little at a time. Beat thoroughly to ensure everything is well-mixed. Spoon into the prepared loaf tin.

Bake in the oven for 40 minutes, then place 2 thin strips of lemon peel on top (avoid removing the cake from the oven – watch you don't burn your hands) and bake in the oven for a further 20 minutes.

Transfer to a wire rack and allow to cool in the tin for at least 20 minutes before turning out. Slice only when completely cold.

# Banana Pizza

This sweet 'pizza' is topped with thickly sliced bananas and a sticky, toffee-like crust of brown sugar and lemon juice. Serve it in wedges with thick clotted cream. Try this as a sweet accompaniment with the Chicken Escalopes on page 75.

Serves  4–6   V  Vegan

**For the base:**
450g strong white flour
1 sachet easy-blend
   dried yeast
½ teaspoon salt
30g caster sugar
2 tablespoons sunflower oil
200–230ml warm water

**For the topping:**
3 large or 4 medium bananas
juice of 1 lemon
60g soft dark brown sugar

For the base, combine the flour, yeast, salt and caster sugar in a large mixing bowl. Make a well in the centre and pour in the oil. Now add just enough warm water to combine to a softish but not sticky dough. Turn on to a floured board and knead for about 10 minutes.

Place in a lightly oiled bowl, cover with clingfilm and leave to rise in a warm place for about 1½ hours, or until well-risen.

Knock back the dough with your fists, then press into an oiled 23 x 33cm Swiss roll tin. Make the dough base as thin as possible, pressing it up the sides of the tin to form a rim.

Lightly cover with clingfilm and place somewhere warm for about 25–30 minutes.

Preheat the oven to 220°C/425°F/gas mark 7. Just before baking, peel the bananas and cut on the diagonal into thick slices. Arrange on top of the dough base, then sprinkle with lemon juice and dark brown sugar.

Bake the pizza in the oven for about 25 minutes, or until the bread rim is puffed up and a golden brown and the bananas are nicely glazed.

Cool for about 10 minutes, then cut into wedges. Serve with clotted cream.

# The Dreaded Soufflé (Lemon Flavour)

There are many horror stories of soufflés not rising, sinking and exploding. This one is very easy, so please don't worry about it. As long as it is light and fluffy, who cares what shape it is? You can try replacing the lemon curd with Nutella and a crushed ripe banana for a different twist. This soufflé makes a fantastic sweet ending to the Potato Rösti on page 84.

Serves   Gluten-free

40g unsalted butter
100g caster sugar, plus 4 teaspoons
4 large eggs, separated
4 tablespoons lemon curd
zest of 4 lemons
icing sugar, to serve

Preheat the oven to 200°C/400°F/gas mark 6. Melt the butter in a small saucepan. Brush four small ramekins in an upward motion with the butter using a pastry brush. Put 1 teaspoon of sugar in each ramekin and roll it around so the inside is coated in sugar. Put them in the fridge.

Mix the egg yolks well with the lemon curd and lemon zest in a large mixing bowl. In a separate clean and dry bowl, whisk the whites using an electric whisk until stiff peaks start to form. Then, still whisking, slowly start adding the sugar. When the whites are at firm peaks (so they stand on their own without flopping over), stop whisking. Gently fold one large spoon of the whisked whites into the yolk and lemon curd mixture. Use a metal spoon to do this, then gradually add the rest until all the whites are folded into the yolks. Do this slowly and don't overwork the mixture.

Spoon the mixture into the buttered and sugared ramekins. Gently tap the ramekins on the work surface so any bubbles rise to the top, and smooth out the mixture with a spatula. Bake in the oven for about 10 minutes until well risen. Try not to open the door while they are cooking. Remove from the oven and sprinkle with icing sugar before serving immediately.

# Strawberry Panettone with Fromage Frais & Honey

Use plump juicy strawberries in season, or bananas in winter, for this simple, satisfying dessert. Try this as a sweet aside after you've served the Quick Walnut & Mushroom Risotto on page 48.

Serves  6

6 slices of panettone or
   brioche
300g strawberries or 3
   bananas, thinly sliced
zest and juice of 1 orange
   or lemon
200ml fromage frais
2 tablespoons clear honey

Preheat the grill to a medium heat and lay the sliced panettone on top of the grill pan. In a large bowl, mix the fruit with the orange or lemon zest and juice and combine gently. Arrange the fruit over the surface of the bread.

Place under the grill and cook until golden and hot – approximately 5–6 minutes.

To serve, slide onto plates, put a generous spoonful of fromage frais in the middle of each, drizzle over the honey and serve immediately.

# Baked
# Apricot Brioche

This dish is a quick take on the much-loved bread and butter pudding, but without the cooking and setting time. It's no harder to prepare than making a quick sandwich. It makes a great pudding alongside Spaghetti with Chilli, Prawns and Parsley on page 59.

Serves  6

1 small brioche loaf or 3
   large croissants
50g unsalted butter, softened
100g apricot jam
2 x 400g cans halved
   apricots in juice
100g golden caster sugar
vanilla ice cream or double
   cream, to serve

Preheat the oven to 200°C/400°F/gas mark 6. Slice the brioche loaf into six thick slices or the croissants in half lengthways and butter on both sides. Lay the slices in an ovenproof dish roughly measuring 20 x 20cm (you may need another brioche loaf to cover the bottom of the dish) and generously spread over the apricot jam.

Drain the apricots (reserving some of the juice) and lay cut-side down onto the buttered and jammed brioche. Sprinkle the sugar over the top and drizzle with 2–3 tablespoons of the reserved apricot juice.

Bake in the oven for 10–15 minutes or until slightly crispy at the edges.

Serve with the accompaniment of your choice.

# Pineapple Kebabs with Vanilla & Maple Syrup

This makes a really good sweet accompaniment with the Naked Burgers on page 72. It is a really straightforward dessert and hot pineapple with cold ice cream and sweet syrup is something very special. This is great cooked on the barbecue if the weather is nice and fantastic served with banana.

Serves

1 supersweet medium-sized pineapple or 2–3 packets of pineapple, pre-cut into chunks
1 teaspoon vanilla paste or 1 vanilla pod
6 tablespoons maple syrup
vanilla ice cream, to serve

Preheat a griddle pan or large frying pan on a medium heat. If you have bought a whole fresh pineapple, you will need to top and tail it. Remove the spiky outer skin using a serrated knife, trying to remove the eyes (brown spots) on the flesh as you go. Cut the pineapple in half, and then cut each half into 4–6 strips. Remove the middle woody core. Push the pineapple strip onto wooden or metal skewers. If you have bought pre-cut pineapple it will be in chunks so push 5–6 pieces onto each skewer.

In a saucepan, mix the vanilla paste or seeds (removed from the pod using a small knife) with the maple syrup and gently heat to a simmer. Brush the syrup onto the pineapple skewers. Lay onto the hot griddle and cook until they start to caramelise. Turn in the pan to ensure they cook and colour evenly. Brush with the syrup as you go. This can also be done under the grill, but you must soak the skewers if you are using wooden ones or they will burn.

Remove from the pan, pour over any remaining syrup and serve with ice cream.

# Blackberry &
# Apple Pears

Quick to prepare and bursting with goodness, this fruit-filled dessert is the perfect end to a midweek supper. Try it served after the Quiche Lorraine on page 32.

Serves  4  GF Gluten-free  V Vegan

4 firm pears, cut in half lengthways and core removed
juice of 1 lemon
1 x 300g can blackberries in natural juice
1 eating apple, cored and chopped
1 teaspoon ground cinnamon
300ml unsweetened apple juice
1 tablespoon cornflour, blended with 2 tablespoons cold water

Preheat the oven to 180°C/350°F/gas mark 4.

Sprinkle the pears with the lemon juice to prevent browning.

Drain the blackberries, reserving the juice. Carefully mix the blackberries with the chopped apple and cinnamon and 2 tablespoons of apple juice. Pile into the centre of each pear half.

Place the pear halves, stuffing side up, in a baking dish and pour over the reserved blackberry juice and remaining apple juice. Bake in the oven for 15-20 minutes until just softened.

Drain the pears, reserving the juice, and keep the pears warm. Mix the juice with the cornflour mixture and heat, stirring constantly, in a small saucepan over a moderate heat until thickened. Serve the pears with the thickened juice and yogurt or fromage frais.

**Variation:** Replace the pears with apricots, either fresh or canned in natural juice.

# INDEX

# Recipe Acknowledgements

We would like to thank the following authors for kind permission to reproduce their recipes:

**Chapter 1: Soups**
p.12 Bubble & Squeak Soup from *Soup* by Nick Sandler & Johnny Acton
p.15 Smoked Turkey & Lentil Soup from *Soup* by Nick Sandler & Johnny Acton
p.16 Coconut & Chicken Soup from *Gorgeous Suppers* by Annie Bell
p.19 Prawn & Pork Wonton Soup from *Soup* by Nick Sandler & Johnny Acton
p.20 Miso Broth with Rice Noodles from *The Modern Vegetarian* by Maria Elia
p.22 Mexican Black Bean Soup from *Soup* by Nick Sandler & Johnny Acton

**Chapter 2: Light Meals**
p.26 Blueberry & Banana Pancakes from *Easy Peasy* by Sophie Wright
pp.28–9 Eggs Benedict from *Ballymaloe Cookery Course* by Darina Allen
p.31 Full Breakfast Frittata from *Homemade* by Clodagh McKenna
p.32 Quiche Lorraine from *Forgotten Skills of Cooking* by Darina Allen
p.34 Asparagus & Spinach Tart from *Classic British Cookbook* edited by Kyle Cathie
p.37 Asparagus, Rocket & Wild Garlic Frittata from *Ballymaloe Cookery Course* by Darina Allen
p.39 Cheese & Mushroom Soufflé from *Classic British Cookbook* edited by Kyle Cathie
p.40 Vegetable Puff Pie from *Classic British Cookbook* edited by Kyle Cathie
p.43 Cruncy Polenta Fishcakes from *The Gluten-free Cookbook* edited by Kyle Cathie
p.45 Pissaladière from *Jekka's Complete Herb Book* by Jekka McVicar
p.47 Peperonata from *Forgotten Skills of Cooking* by Darina Allen
p.48 Quick Walnut & Mushroom Risotto from *Easy Italian in Minutes* edited by Kyle Cathie
p.51 Pasta with Ham & Vegetable Sauce from *The Gluten-free Cookbook* edited by Kyle Cathie
p.52 Tortilla with Chorizo from *Gorgeous Suppers* by Annie Bell

**Chapter 3: Hearty Dishes**
p.56 Lemon Chicken with Lemon & Sage Risotto from *Easy Italian in Minutes* edited by Kyle Cathie
p.59 Spaghetti with Chilli, Prawns & Parsley from *Ballymaloe Cookery Course* by Darina Allen
p.60 Creamy Macaroni with Smoked Bacon from *Homemade* by Clodagh McKenna
p.63 Pasta with Sardines, Pine Nuts & Raisins *Ballymaloe Cookery Course* by Darina Allen
p.64 Spaghetti Puttanesca from *Gorgeous Suppers* by Annie Bell

## Chapter 4: Vegetarian Delights

## Chapter 5: Sweet Endings

# Photography Acknowledgements

We would like to thank the following photographers for kind permission to reproduce their images:

p.2, p. 4–5, p.6, p.7, p.9 William Reavell

**Chapter 1: Soups**
p.13, p.14 William Reavell
p.17 Chris Alack from *Gorgeous Suppers* by Annie Bell
p.18 William Reavell
p.21 Jonathan Gregson from *Modern Vegetarian* by Maria Elia
p.23 William Reavell

**Chapter 2: Light Meals**
p.27 Kate Whitaker from *Easy Peasy* by Sophie Wright
p.29 William Reavell
p.30 Alberto Peroli from *Homemade* by Clodagh McKenna
p.33 Peter Cassidy from *Forgotten Skills of Cooking* by Darina Allen
p.34 Gus Filgate from *Classic British Cookbook* edited by Kyle Cathie
p.37 William Reavell
p.38, p.41 Gus Filgate from *Classic British Cookbook* edited by Kyle Cathie
p.42 Gus Filgate from The *Gluten-free Cookbook* edited by Kyle Cathie
p.45 Jekka McVicar from *Jekka's Complete Herb Book*
p.46 William Reavell
p.49 Gus Filgate from *Easy Italian in Minutes* edited by Kyle Cathie
p.50 Gus Filgate from The *Gluten-free Cookbook* edited by Kyle Cathie
p.53 Chris Alack from *Gorgeous Suppers* by Annie Bell

**Chapter 3: Hearty Dishes**
p.57 Gus Filgate from *Easy Italian in Minutes* edited by Kyle Cathie
p.58, p.61, p.62 William Reavell
p.65, p.66 Chris Alack from *Gorgeous Suppers* by Annie Bell
p.69 Romas Foord from *Home at 7, Dinner at 8* by Sophie Wright
p.70 Alberto Peroli from *Homemade* by Clodagh McKenna
p.73 William Reavell
p.74 Chris Alack from *Gorgeous Suppers* by Annie Bell
p.77, p.78, p.81 Gus Filgate from *Classic British Cookbook* edited by Kyle Cathie

**Chapter 4: Vegetarian Delights**

p.85, p.86 William Reavell
p.89 Steve Lee from *Seriously Good! Gluten-free Cooking* by Phil Vickery
p.90 Kate Whitaker from *Easy Peasy* by Sophie Wright
p.93, p.94 William Reavell
p.97 Romas Foord from *Home at 7, Dinner at 8* by Sophie Wright
p.98 Chris Alack from *Gorgeous Suppers* by Annie Bell
p.101 Gus Filgate from The *Gluten-free Cookbook* edited by Kyle Cathie

**Chapter 5: Sweet Endings**

p.105 Gus Filgate from *Classic British Cookbook* edited by Kyle Cathie
p.106, p.109, p.110 William Reavell
p.113 Gus Filgate from *Easy Italian in Minutes* edited by Kyle Cathie
p.114, p.117 Romas Foord from *Home at 7, Dinner at 8* by Sophie Wright
p.118 Gus Filgate from *The Gluten-free Cookbook* edited by Kyle Cathie